Life
Presented
In
Verse

Laurie Wilkinson
The Psychy Poet

This edition published in Great Britain in 2017 by MyVoice Publishing

www.MyVoicePublishing.com

ISBN 978-1-909359-56-7

Cover Photo: The author without a glass in his hand, contrary to rumour.

Photo by Lucy Carnagan
http://lucycarnaghanphotography.zenfolio.com

Introduction

Well here we are again, somewhat even more unbelievably, with book 5 in just over 3 years as of now, mid June 2017.

As I keep writing my poems then I will produce the books, which people have kindly told me they very much look forward to. I have now written at this time about 350 poems in three and a half years!

It does seem though thankfully, that my quality is continually endorsed, as on 31/7/2017 another two of my poems are again for national publication by Forward Poetry. This will make a total of six now included in different books of theirs in three years, and will again go into the national finals that they run.

With these six then, and my own five published books now, my son was prompted to joke and ask "if I was starting my own private library"?

I must say I am particularly proud of this current book that you are now reading, as apart from 70 new poems, I have included the six published from the national finals mentioned above, and on request have also put in some favourites from my previous four books too.

I always love it when people tell me of their own particular favourite poem that means something special for them, as well as many others resonating as well. Some of these poems have "sold books" on their own, so check the Appendix to see if you agree.....

Meanwhile I continue to do "reading gigs", and various fundraising for my supported charity Help for Heroes, that all book sales donate to, alongside money from my "Commissioned Poem for You" service for relatives, events and business advertising verse as well.

I will whisper this next bit quietly, as before you read this I think my mischievous house mates Ted and Beth who feature in many "Humour" section poems, including several in this book, will have their "dreamed of" Fan Club, possibly on Facebook!

To check on this and all my activities I now have a website www.psychypoet.com with regular Blog Posts, as well as my Facebook page "The Psychy Poet Laurie Wilkinson", please do check them out!

Please now enjoy exploring this new book which follows the same style and themes of previous books, thus will certainly have something special for you and more, alongside all the other poems that people kindly feed back, resonate many thoughts of theirs on our lives and the world. As ever, "The Journey Continues".....

Laurie Wilkinson Bsc (hons) RMN

Acknowledgements

Having just read my acknowledgements in my fairly recent fourth book, only published in December 2016, I noticed that I said I would try to avoid repetition. Even harder now with this fifth book so quickly following that one, so I will attempt to be succinct, whilst hopefully not missing anybody out!

I do again though need to recognise great and increased support and encouragement from family and friends, and my usual "supportive suspects" in the various groups and organisations I belong to.

Thus thanks again to the 42ⁿᵈ Highland Regiment (1815), The Napoleonic Association, Anderida Writers Eastbourne, The South East and Eastbourne area "Mumpreneurs", all terrific friends on my French Mobile Home site, The Sussex Newspaper Online & sister paper Bonjour France Online that allow me to write my monthly articles. Many other local East Sussex businesses, shops, pubs, charities and great people I liaise with too numerous to mention individually by name.

I must however acknowledge a a few special folks for their amazing support, so again Joanne P from Wales, a "book seller extraordinary", Mick W Senior, Joanna of Vines Flowers Westham, Sharon W of Olive Design, The Garden Bar Eastbourne Waterfront for their continued donations and help from my beginning! Liz and Ben P Seabreeze Cleaning, Lesley A T, a colleague from the past, recently back to be both a great helper and supporter. Many more must remain unmentioned but not forgotten here as you will be thanked elsewhere and perhaps personally......

Again My Voice Publishing need a mention, with now James H alongside the regular team who "suffer and indulge" me as a probably "too over enthusiastic", but determined and growing poetic author!

As ever my final recognition of gratitude is to people taking the time to read this book, and with an even bigger thanks to the kind folks who have bought my previous books, and buy this one too, which as ever ensures my donation to the excellent charity Help for Heroes from all my sales.

Life Presented in Verse

Experiences of life come to us all
Though some will prefer not to see,
But there can be no hiding place
And that's up to folks like me.

Who will observe and then present
All that life will bring to us.
From laughter and tears, to death,
To confront without a fuss.

For everyone of us will experience
Good and bad that we don't choose.
So how we react and deal with this,
Will decide if we win or lose.

Contents

ROMANCE

Love Cruise

I've often heard it said by people
You easily fall in love when afloat,
So maybe we should take the hint
And get ourselves on a boat,
A ship or perhaps cruise liner,
That can bring on amorous fun
For most would probably enjoy it
After all is said and done.

The sailors smart in their uniforms
Ladies gorgeous with flowing hair,
And the rocking motion of the ship
Can lead the willing to a lair.
But best be warned in advance
That all voyages have to end,
So whispered promises on board
On land may cease to blend.

Of course there are many waters
With some shallow, others deep,
And unless you are compliant
No love harvest will you reap.
Thus best to set off and away
To cruise across those seas,
With open mind, and hopeful soul
And a warm heart that agrees.

--ooOoo--

Ease of Entry

When you apply your magic touch
You take my breath away,
And take me to loves deep feelings
That don't need shades of grey.
For it's as if you have ease of entry
To me, without need of a key.
Though that's no great mystery,
Just your unique chemistry.

So touch away sweet lady
For you have an open goal,
And an unobstructed free way
Straight into my very soul.

Though I don't think I would protest
Even if I possibly could,
Because I'm certain that no-one
Can ever be so very good
As you are, when with me,
In all our glorious connections.
For no architect of life
Could ever plan such erections,
As our love and life together
That cannot be pulled apart.
So we will travel roads together
Just living off one heart.

Now I know that there are doubters,
Maybe jealous of our ecstasy.
But they've probably never felt
Just what you do for me,
Or perhaps I do for you too.
If all I see in your release,
Causes such deep sensations
To give us inner peace.

--ooOoo--

Blindspot

Solid foundations can crumble
As a solid structure quakes,
When love crashes into lives
With the vibrations that it makes.
For a complete stranger may suddenly
Cause childish behaviours to show.
When for no apparent reason
They arouse feelings you don't know.

As something about them haunts
Some deep and inner thought,
That you only have at those times
When desire and lust are caught
Seeping into your own world,
And giving such a lonely view,
So are shattered dramatically
When emotions awake you.

With bright eyes alluring gleam
And ocean depths revealing,
Every attraction you can't resist
As your defences all start peeling.
So you feel completely naked
To those beautiful probing eyes,
As you recoil in shocked confusion
And can speak no words, just sighs.

For if you can believe in this
Miracle of attractions glow,
You never know when you will fall
Under magic moments flow
To take you on a journey,
Though you may not move too far
As your dreamy loving muse
Just wants you as you are!

--ooOoo--

Coincidental Chance

You spoke to me out of the blue
And I didn't know who you were,
But like Pitney's "24 hours from Tulsa"
Such happenings can occur.
For I had felt an instant shudder
That I couldn't quite control,
Also a strange realisation
You had touched my very soul.

We did the awkward introductions
That two strangers muddle through,
After your identity mistake
That I was someone else you knew.
So I tried to cover your blushes
And embarrassment so clear,
But again I felt compelled
By the need to hold you near.

Thus we both stood quite flustered
By clearly felt sensations,
Running through the two of us
Defying all explanations,
As to what had just happened
Within an amazing heartbeat,
When people blend together
And their very souls now meet.

Now you look at me and say my name
And I go shaky at the knees,
But when I felt your touch
I thought my blood would freeze.
So now we need to decipher
Just what we can understand
About this, and further actions,
As we walk off, hand in hand.

--ooOoo--

Picture

When I contemplate a painting
I always think of you,
Pretty as any art work
And so lovely with it too.
For no Mona Lisa picture
Or da Vinci at his best,
Could ever create attraction
That could ever pass your test.

For brush strokes can't come alive
However clever is the touch,
And inner and outer beauty
Will always need so much
To capture all its presentation,
Only fully blossomed in the flesh
That no painting can fully copy
Or have a scent so fresh.

Thus a living breathing person
Is real beauty to behold,
So however warm a painting looks,
When you touch it, it feels cold.

Thus indulge any masterpiece
That you may have for real,
As you are truly a collector
With your picture you can feel.

So when appraising your treasure
Of art in human form,
Don't ever take it for granted
Or believe it's just the norm.
For you must love and cultivate
Your own Mona Lisa smile,
Remembering you have it always
And not for just a while.

--ooOoo--

Eye Line Smile

It doesn't take much to lift a heart
Or cause our head to swoon.
Just loving words or chaste kiss,
Can lift us round the moon.

Whether eyes are dark or light
They can twinkle and bewitch,
Causing a thrill right through you
As if someone clicked a switch.

Seeing can makes hearts flutter
With pulses racing with a touch.
There is no magic spell for this,
Just that we love so very much.

Contented sighs descend on us
Like some heaven sent cascade.
And nothing will keep us apart,
Even rivers, hill or barricade!

A plain face may cause sunrise
When it breaks into a smile,
And when that beam is loving
Joy will fast flow like the Nile!

Whether eyes are dark or light
They can twinkle and bewitch,
And if they sparkle just for you
Your whole life will enrich.
For in a world that's tough at times
Where you strive hard for reward,
Being drawn to loving eyes
May bring ecstatic life accord!

--ooOoo--

Soft Touch

You have a very special touch
That's both soft and sincere,
And I must confess to melting
The moment you are near.
So what is the big difference
From other women I have known?
Perhaps it's allure and chemistry
That are your very own.

I can still remember well
How it was once with you,
When you made darkness light
And all my fuses blew,
As you weaved your sensual magic
That I never could resist.
But why does it linger on when
You're not the only one I've kissed?

So looking back I still smile
At the thoughts of how we'd been,
Laughing with a love and desire
That never could be obscene.
For I know your hands were soft
As you applied your loving touch,
With the opening of your body
That I used to love so much.

But they were in the mists of time
That have sadly passed by now,
Leaving just the memories
Of our where, when and how.
Though I still recall your soft touch
Turning my emotions into fire,
And made my being just for you
When you turned the heat up higher!

--ooOoo--

Volunteer

It is often said that a volunteer
Is worth more than ten pressed men,
Of course now that includes women
But wasn't always a factor then.
Now women have an equal say
So can make more decisions too,
About the challenges of life
And what you want to do.

One meaning of a volunteer
Is about someone freely choosing,
To help out, or give their time
Instead of just idly cruising,
Without an idea or plan
Of what you want to achieve.
So being around helping others
Your pattern you can weave.

For volunteers gain experience
Like the requirements of the world,
And business skills and attitudes
That need to be unfurled,
Dealing with different people
Will always give you thrills,
And trying different challenges
Is sure to teach new skills.

So don't dither about wondering
How to get that special job,
For learning things as a volunteer
Will make your life blood throb!

--ooOoo--

The Messenger

The messenger calls as usual
And you take it as always read,
But you may get a shock
When worrying that he's dead.

For he hasn't called, or spoke
So you wonder what is wrong?
But maybe nothing is for him,
When he sings another's song,
Just how they like to hear him
As for her he speaks so well.
So you've faded in his memory,
Though not that you can tell.

As like thunder, the silence roars
Reverberating about your ears,
That once rejoiced to hear him
But now noise is replaced by tears
Of an acid recrimination,
That you didn't cherish it all.
And thus you have lost it now
Even if begging him to call!

So your messenger has vanished
And seems won't be coming back,
To pick up all the pieces
That crumble as you crack.

For no messages are forthcoming,
As the delivery man has gone.
Leaving you with a hard lesson,
About the man who shone
That bright light in your life,
And always made you smile.
But when felt you gave nothing
He knew you weren't his style.

--ooOoo--

Faint Heart

In our lives I'm sure we've all heard
That "so and so" is big trouble,
With often the rumour or gossip spread
By the person who is a double
Of the very one they're on about,
And calling the nasty name.
So how ironic that it transpires
That they are just the same.

Now there are both men and women
Who don't do so well in love,
So the warning off of these
Could be guidance from above.
Now I have to recount for me
That such a lady did arrive.
And I dived in despite concerns,
But still managed to survive.

And oh so very much more than that
As my whole body danced and sang,
Which would all have passed me by
If I heeded the alarms that rang
Out from lots of would-be helpers
All worried about my fate.
So I can only joyously report
That I found a happy state.

For this lady who I was warned of
In recounted stories of spite,
Was not at all how she was described
And was in fact a great delight.
So we spent many ecstatic days
Sadly unable to be followed through,
Thus take care about people's warnings
As next time it may be you.

--ooOoo--

Cradle to the Grave

A lilting voice from the past
That will affect you like no other.
Bringing love and goose bumps too,
For it can only be your mother.

The one who always from your birth
Stood by you with no quaking,
Though inside she cried bitter tears
If bad decisions you were making,
Or was given cause to be upset
At your failure to return the love,
Which will always be too late
After she is taken to live above.

For a mother always looks with pride
At your first shaky steps to walk,
Across your rocky paths in life
Since she first helped you to talk.
Thus had also been there for you
From that cradle to the grave,
Watching out for all those dangers
As your soul she tried to save.

So when others reject and doubt you
Your doting mother will be there,
To ensure she can protect you
With unconditional loving care,
That first began when as a child
You needed succour and a kiss,
Given with uncomplaining lips
You will always sorely miss.

A lilting voice from the past
You will remember all your years,
Though may not always appreciate
Until her passing brings your tears.
So while you have her, be ever nice
To your solid embracing fir,
Who whatever heartbreak you cause
Will still put you first, before her.

--ooOoo--

Feeling Special

When we're together I am somewhere
But lost and nowhere when I'm alone,
For with you I can skip and cartwheel
Though if apart my heart's a stone!

So secretly I'll be your personal ghost
All around, watching with my stare,
I am the out breath, when in you breathe
And I'm the wind that blows your hair.
Thus note the trembling at your sleeve
And feel the itch you cannot scratch,
Because I'm the warm light that shines
Like darkness lit by a match!

When we're together I am somewhere
But lost and nowhere when I'm alone,
For with you I can skip and cartwheel
Though if apart my heart's a stone!

Should you feel sensation at your blouse
Or some finite movement at your skirt,
And heartbeats move to unfelt rhythm
It's just me protecting you from hurt.
Be not afraid when you see a shadow
Or feel a touch, moth like at the ear,
It's just my presence come to love you
And ensure safe passages you steer!

So have no fear of the world around you
Even lightning strikes from above,
For you're safe within an armour
Fashioned by my spirits love.

--ooOoo--

Fake

Some things that we meet in life
Are just fake and counterfeit.
Though we may not always know,
For they can sorely test our wit.
Whether friends, gems or paintings
The results are just as bad,
But for me the worst is with people
As I find that so very sad.

For there's not much else so tragic
Or debilitating to us all.
As when somebody lures you on,
Purposely to make you fall,
Into a false and cruel game
Where only the genuine lose.
Because of crafty, evil cunning
Contrived by a callous ruse,
To get you to open up
Giving all your secrets out.
So they can be used against you
And they will, without a doubt!

For some new affections are a trap
Set by the uncaring and the smart,
Who are completely void of conscience
And will probably have no heart.

But don't be too down heartened
For these manipulators are rare,
And you can meet many honest folk
Who can make your heart a pair.
Thus just be very careful
About all the moves you make,
For if your guts give out a warning
Then they probably are a fake.

--ooOoo--

Message from the Heart

Eyes can only see and admire
Objects of wonder in their views,
Especially when widened in awe
At a stunning hoped-for muse.

So an alert goes through the body
With the blood streaming around,
With an awakened amorous idea
That a gorgeous siren's been found.
But we have little control over this
And must obey it from the start,
Within this "action stationed" frame
Hearing this message from the heart.

All people and the sights once seen
Have now faded from your sight,
Reduced to mere bit-part players
By this seismic feelings might.

Now the brain will try to balance
These vibrations, so very strong,
But the senses now have a target
Though the brain thinks it's wrong.

Thus now nervous and infantile
A besotted body makes its move.
With new and aroused emotions
That the brain tries to approve.
So embarkations to possible grief
By the heart are now fully set
Off onwards, to hoped for passions
With this siren, very newly met.

--ooOoo--

Ted n Beth's Delight

Ted and Beth are ecstatic bears
Having finally achieved their aim,
For they're going to have a Fan Club
Of their own , and in their name.
It may soon be launched on Facebook,
And have some teddy-news space
On The Psychy Poet's website,
With their own Fan Club's place!

And perhaps they really should now
Have that little extra bit of fame,
As they have their very own video
Thus have not been quite the same,
Since it's been seen on social media
And even on YouTube too.
With a poem published nationally
They scarce can believe it's true.

But the evidence is all out there
In their "Poet Dad's five books,
Featuring Ted's wit and brain
Alongside Beth's dark good looks.
The poems also do record though
Flooding the house and Ted's snoring,
Them missing breakfast, and dancing
For they never will be boring.

So all in all for Ted and Beth
It's been a fun-filled learning curve.
And I have to finally accept now,
A Fan Club they Deserve!

--ooOoo--

Pride and Joy

Despite many concerns expressed
I shared time with a certain lady,
Although I had heard misgivings
That she could be somewhat shady.
But always one to jump in head first
Where angels fear to tread,
I got involved with mixed emotions
And found a paradise instead.

For there were exclusive qualities
That I found this lady had,
And to my extreme pleasure
There were far more good than bad.
As she took a special interest
Into what I said I enjoyed,
And so undertook an active role
On how they could be employed.

Of course I not being one to rest
Upon laurels and joys given to me,
Reciprocated with fervent endeavour
To ensure that she could see,
And indeed to feel as well
All the sensations that I felt.
So we had a complete togetherness
That worried concerns would melt.

Thus very contented times ensued
In both of our lives and actions,
For when it came to giving love
Neither of us did it by fractions.
Which only goes to show
It is not always wise to heed,
Rumours or worries of others
As you won't know where they lead.

--ooOoo--

Unknown Journey

The very beauty of the gift
Was that it was not seen or showing,
We did not know or notice
That something great was growing.

You sailed in your ship, I in mine,
No other course was charted.
We journeyed on across our seas
Unaware just what had started.

I did not know but I looked for you,
Your way, your eyes, your smile.
A touch can take our breath away
And be felt from near a mile.

But the greatest star was yet to shine
Beaming light from sky to sea.
I was manic, laughing , flying
When you said you cared for me!

--ooOoo--

Spark

To have a spark for life is vital
To gain fulfilment true,
And a sense of achievement
With the many things you do.

For though all people have one
Some are left to wilt and die,
Or because they're lost in sorrow
Will drown and cannot try
To combust or kick start life
That lives in an empty shell,
For only flints that keep sparking
Can help us truly to excel.

But some people become jaded
And wearied by their road,
With heavy heart and failing soul
They've collapsed beneath their load,
So no longer have their spark
Or make any attempt to rise,
Which will only bring contempt
For someone who never tries.

--ooOoo--

Back Pass

As I contemplate the world
I must also consider then.
How would I be received,
If I passed this way again?
For unlike the famous saying
We only pass this way one time,
That was more on our whole life
Rather than a local climb.

So back to my conjecture
Of how would I be perceived,
If returning to past haunts
Would I still be well received?
Well certainly I have never
Done anything criminal or dire,
That could be held against me
And cause a greeting to expire.

As I have always tried to live
By not wanting to wear a crown,
And always nice to people going up
I might meet coming down.
And with my other true motto
Possibly the best I ever had,
For if you can't do a good turn,
Then don't do one that's bad.

Thus I really like to think
Happily and with some sway,
That I would be quite welcome
Should I return this way.
For people often mention my laugh
And say I have a ready smile,
But just to be on the safe side
I'll be good for a little while.

--ooOoo--

Trinket

A trinket is an ornament or memento
That is of little value and worth.
But could possibly get sentimental
If allied to a special birth,
Or something that's held dear
Becoming an intrinsic part of you.
But mostly the trinket is worthless
Whatever you feel or do.

So why then do we collect them?
When not wanted until seen,
With the initial attraction to them
That soon made us very keen,
To get and own these items
Which we succumbed to and bought,
Though now lay about forgotten
Without a second thought.

Because far more important in life
Are the lovely people there,
With you to make those memories
And wonderful days you share.
So when without a thought or plan
A chance meeting turns to bliss,
That without a shadow of doubt
You wouldn't want to miss.

So going back to our trinkets
And maybe other things we get,
Which cannot hold a candle
To that someone special met.

Who fills our life with sunshine
Even when it's a cloudy day.
For a person to love and treasure
Is a far better gift and way,
To find life's joys and wonder
That a trinket could never do,
As the simple fact of the matter
Is that love is best for you!

--ooOoo--

Jigsaw

Dreamy figures of great delight
All come dancing into view,
I have a panorama of beauty
But know what I must do.

For you have made intrusions
Seismic like upon my soul,
As we determine to be together
Making our separate pieces whole,
Like some closely fitting jigsaw
That a glorious picture makes,
For it had become quite desperate
To complete for both our sakes.

I can still see your posture
With majestic desire for me,
That I had to return with vigour
How it was designed to be.
Now disappearing from all else
Except the views fixed in our sight,
We released basic desires
With erupting volcano might.

So now our jigsaw was complete
And you in your ecstasy cried,
Whilst we had flown together
Returning to land satisfied.

--ooOoo--

HUMOUR

Bar Room Star

Every pub or bar will have one
There are lots of them about,
And while everyone likes talking
He feels the need to shout.

Amongst his group of cronies
He must be the loudest bloke,
Then burst into raucous laughter
Every time he cracks a joke!

I turn my head to see him
But you couldn't miss the noise,
For he's the best at shouting
In the group of loud old boys.

We all laugh at something
In our own personal way,
Within the bounds of reason
As appropriate for the day.

But this loud man doesn't realise
His grating voice won't nestle,
And he clearly has forgotten
The saying of the empty vessel.

So the loud man's noise continues
And his voice you couldn't douse,
Though I have a deep suspicion
That at home he's like a mouse!

--ooOoo--

Badgers

There now appears to be a rash
Of job-description I D cards,
Worn proudly by those workers
Keen not to be seen as retards.

For they nobly masquerade now
Behind a "managers" badge bold.
Until of course you make a request
When they will just do as they are told,
By someone with a much larger badge
Or just metaphorically worn.
But clearly a step above the first,
Now gawping fish-like and forlorn.

At their forbidden rule to answer
The very simplest question asked,
But every dog must know its place
And not try to be multi-tasked.

I even see now that these cards
Are on ribbons dangled from the neck,
On view as a false security
For any requested check.

Though I really can't stop laughing
At such a futile little gesture,
For any would-be villain now
Couldn't be bothered to pester,
For a "Poundland" type of I D card
That could be "knocked up" in a shed.
As they would just hack the laptops
For any security breach instead.

But now even on holiday sites
Ribbon badges are flourished to see,
Exactly who has "weighed and paid"
But don't give one to me.

As I have never liked tick boxes
That we can all be placed in.
So carry my driving licence card
In my wallet, to avoid the sin,
Of a total non-conforming breed
Which may be a bridge too far.
But fear not for if I want something
I know exactly who you are!

--ooOoo--

Pardon?

Can't take your call at the moment
The metallic voice intones,
And will repeat this basic sentence
Every time that someone phones.
Please leave your message then
After you hear the beep,
So that we can get back to you
And this promise they will keep.

Well, that is on the condition
That you got their number right,
For metallic lady could be anyone
As no name, or face was in sight.
Thus I'm sure I'm not alone
In leaving a message for reply,
To someone that I didn't know
Who will sit and wonder why!

For I like to hear a real voice
Perhaps recorded by a friend,
Or a person saying who you rang
At the phones other end,
As a posh, plastic recording
Could be anyone wrongly dialled,
So now I will always ring again
Ensuring the number is re trialled.

Though it doesn't just end there,
For when the person rings you back
You could be out or busy,
So your voice they will lack.
And so your message will talk to them
Just as theirs had spoken to you,
For if you want to feel important
This is what you need to do.

So sometimes in a few minutes
You could ring many different folk,
And get all their answer-phones
Which really is a joke.
For you must await a return call,
But perhaps all this was staged,
For if you try to ring again,
That number's now engaged.

Thus on and on it all goes round
A circle of messages in a store.
But by then you've had enough
And metallic lady's the last straw!

--ooOoo--

Colour Bar

A multicoloured Lycra suit
With a crash helmet on the head,
Could have been the "Tour de France"
And not a narrow lane instead.

With heads tucked down low
And bums all highly raised
To try and cut a second off,
So cycling gods will be praised.
But any poor motorist trying
To overtake the rainbow team,
Will just have to sit and wait
Behind their bright slipstream.

Thus an obvious question to ask
About the clear bike path nearby
That is a much safer route,
So why won't the "Lycra Lot" try
To use this specific facility
For them, as they race in a pack?
Instead of blocking up the road
Where frustrated motorists stack.

But I do fear this is clearly lost,
On the cyclists with sunglasses
Under those protective cycle hats,
To ensure that nothing passes
By their puffing, pumping group,
Swarming like manic bees,
Moving together in a sweaty horde
Whilst everyone else must freeze.

Though of course everyone has a right
To enjoy how they want to play.
But when it's a needless roadblock,
Get out the bloody way!

--ooOoo--

Sample

At certain ages our NHS
Want to do tests on us,
They say that they're simple
And sure to cause no fuss.
Well it said that in my letter
That came with all the kit,
To take the samples from me
To check that I was fit.

Now I do accept the importance
Of finding any "nasties" early,
But I really wasn't prepared
For the collecting hurly burly,
With the need to take samples
From a normal bodily motion.
Although it wasn't really that,
Causing the most commotion.

For the naturally passed stool
Mustn't touch the toilet water,
So you have to prevent this
In a battle with no quarter!

Thus I readily placed my trap,
That my clever brain had thought
Would do the job in hand,
But no motion did get caught.
For it was heavier than my tray
I had contrived to do the task.
So this job needs experience
But who the hell do you ask?

Well I decided there was nobody,
I could ask about catching poo.
So I had to rack my brains,
To see just what to do.
And the idea I had was good,
Putting something on the bend.
For I successfully caught my prize
That with my sticks I could attend.

So with a scrape at one end
And another bit from the rest,
I did this for the five days
Then sent away my test,
Sealed neatly in the little bag
And put in a post box near.
So you can imagine my relief
When my tests came back clear.

For it wasn't just the clean bill
My health had without stain,
More the great joy of not needing
To have to do it all again!

--ooOoo--

Beth's Slippers

Beth bear likes carpet slippers
And loves to wear her mums,
But has to remove them quickly
Whenever her mum comes
Back into the house again,
From a trip to the local shop.
Beth knows she shouldn't do it
Though finds it hard to stop.

Now Ted has told Beth off
About her foot comfort greed.
Saying bears don't want footwear,
Though Beth just finds the need
To feel those comfy slippers
All warm around her paws,
But wouldn't wear them outside
As they're only for indoors.

But Beth got a big shock
When next the slippers wore,
For they were worn and smelly
And can't be put on any more.
So she whispered to her dad
To give mum a special treat,
And buy brand new slippers
For the comfort of her feet.

So Beth's mum now has new ones
Nice and comfortable to wear,
That although meant for humans
Are most appealing to our bear.
Though Beth now has to be good
And for her naughtiness atone,
But I hate to see her unhappy
So bought a pair to be her own.

--ooOoo--

Dress Sense

There is a tricky problem
To avoid an awkward sight,
When men consider their dressing
On the left or to the right.
So choice of clothing is important
And they mustn't be too tight,
Or you will be clearly showing
If you prefer the left or right.

But baggy trousers aren't the answer
Even if you are contrite.
For loose fittings may well choose
If you're going left or right.
Or may even cause a nuisance
And perhaps a concerning fight,
If attempting to stay central
And not on left or right.

Thus for men to feel more relaxed
With non worrying delight,
They must have a confidence
Of not causing sudden fright,
With an accidental display
Even if it's only very slight,
So all must firmly be in place
To the left or to the right.

Though now in enlightened times
Where rules are black and white,
You shouldn't get into trouble
Or put anyone to flight.
In fact possibly the opposite
Which can make your future bright,
If your dressing is more obvious
And brings an invite for the night.

--ooOoo--

First Sex Lessons

We had no sex education at school
Or any that I can remember well.
Just about the gender differences
And hair growing where you tell,
What each other's parts look like
As there were no diagrams to see,
What boy and girls are like
And the different ways to pee.

We did have girls in my class though,
Who would pose and do their best
To help us, particularly Angela
Keen to show off her growing chest.
Though I wasn't too taken with it
Shown in the chemistry room with tubes,
For she was less impressively large
Than "Fat Barry's" large boy boobs!

But there was an unofficial lesson
Though it was actually called P T,
Where we had to strip off in the gym
And girls navy bloomers we could see.
Though again it made little impression
At my young and tender years,
But I have seen in much later times
They reduce some old men to tears.

Thus probably my main sex education
Was when older boys did arrange
A look at Janice the girl next door,
Though it all seemed rather strange,
When she pulled down her panties
To show us a hairy slope and mole.
But being football mad back then,
I failed to see another game and goal.

So that was all school days taught
On how these gender mysteries grow,
With odd things happening down there
That at first you didn't want to know.
So you just carried on with sport
Until soon needing to learn about
A growing interest in girls bodies,
With all the fun of finding out!

--ooOoo--

O M G!

One of the most overused prattles now
Must be the "oh my god" saying,
Often said many times in a row
And has nothing to do with praying.
Probably another modern influence
That has been picked up here,
And garbled nonsensically too
In a manner not sincere.

Sometimes like a collective chorus
Uttered by a multi sized throng,
And certainly not an "hallelujah" one
Or Hebrew slaves going wrong.
But "oh my god" is now universal
And can be intoned at will,
Which will grate on sensitive ears
Far worse if the voice is shrill.

But I grew up with sayings too
Though I think much more in keeping,
To the area I came from
Where our humour wasn't sleeping.
Things like "oh stack me sweetly"
Have a more poetic ring,
Than the often repeated "oh my god"
That a tired boredom will bring.

So an exclamation of "Gordon Bennett!"
Or a rude one about "blue bums",
For me have much more magic,
When out of my mouth it comes,
With another long term favourite
That has an amusing ring,
When shouted in pained frustration
You "cow son" blooming thing!

Thus I still believe the old gems
Will always be the best,
When "oh my god" has been forgotten
And can no longer pass the test,
Of muttered exclamations
When we're surprised or frustrated.
So keep those old sayings safe
As they really are gold plated.

--ooOoo--

Knickers

Knickers are very evocative
And mean something to nearly all,
Though some people prefer them big
Whilst others like them small.

There are people always trying
To get in them, others out,
While bashful keep them firmly on
Many people will have a doubt,
Just which knickers to wear
Or even if they should,
Get into this undergarment game
If they intend to just be good.

And we must remember too
That advice given by our mums,
To always wear clean underwear
In case we show our bums,
After being in an accident
That can befall mankind,
But if you end up in hospital
There's much more on your mind.

For if this accident is very bad
And your brain now hardly flickers,
You'll have much more to worry about
Than the condition of your knickers.
Though in other situations
When you really can't be sure
If your luck is going to be in,
Less, could then be more.

So perhaps we should give more thought
About how our underwear fits,
Because it could be more important
Than just material to cover bits.

--ooOoo--

Tea for Two

Now Ted and Beth like a cup of tea
And will drink it all day long,
But both are reluctant to make it
So that's where it all goes wrong.

For Ted will say it's Beth's turn
She of course says it's Ted's,
So before you can say "teddy bear"
Another disagreement spreads
Into a mini bear fight,
Although they mean no harm.
For Beth will use her female wiles
And Ted will be all charm.

Thus often I am the peacemaker
And also the tea-making man.
Whilst they have their little bicker,
Though I suspect it's all the plan.
With a very cunning teddy ruse
To get me to make their drink,
But although I go along with it
I'm not as silly as they think!

For every time I make their tea
And we sit drinking with a chat.
I find out all their secrets,
How they got up to this and that.
For although they are a lovely pair
And our hearts they do enslave,
They can still be quite mischievous
So I make sure they behave.

Thus our little tea drinking parties
Have an agenda for me too.
As they help me keep a close eye,
On just what they plan to do!

--ooOoo--

Full Frontal Folly

I love me, I'm handsome and fantastic
So up there with the best I rate,
Though if I'm brutally honest
I've passed my "best by" date.
But like so many other people
Maybe I try to deny this truth,
So will be careful with photographs
As I'm no longer a mere youth.

So many attractive attributes
Like my athleticism and hair.
Are largely gone, like other folks,
Though some don't seem to care.
And so will post real close ups
On social media for all those,
Who whoop and say "how beautiful"
And laughing, look up your nose.

Though of course this a personal choice
Albeit probably the wrong pick,
For despite others nagging doubts
To these "full frontals" they will stick,
And put themselves in the limelight
Hoping that everyone will fawn,
"Oh you're gorgeous" and suchlike
When in truth they smirk and yawn.

For like other indulgent projections
That push themselves onto centre stage,
I too love myself completely
But still accept and recognise my age.
So maybe you should take more care
And be like the elegant giraffe,
For despite folks affectionate squeals
Most are having a good laugh.

So although I'm not suggesting now
That when older you should hide,
But just recommending caution
As delusions outweigh pride.

--ooOoo--

Nimble Paws

Now despite being quite mischievous
Some things Ted and Beth keep quiet.
As they like to have some secrets
And not always want to run riot,
Or cause any playful chaos
That mostly they will do.
So I will whisper they like dancing
But that's between me and you.

Thus Beth likes the slow sensual
Movements of the waltz,
While Ted loves the flamboyance
Of a dramatic dance of course.
So while Beth will slink around
With Ted counting one, two, three,
He much prefers the lively tango
And cavorts for all to see.

But naturally they have to practice
And that is how I caught them out,
Sneaking in to see unnoticed
Both Ted's strut, and Beth's pout.

Though I made sure I wasn't caught
So can have another crafty look,
At those lovable, naughty bears
Learning their dancing from a book.
But meanwhile I love to tease them
And they don't know what to say,
When I creep up behind them
With a loud shout of "ole!"

--ooOoo--

Bear in the Window

The teddy bear was hanging
By it's neck inside the shop,
So I walked right in to tell them
That I had to make it stop.

A woman came to serve me
So I pointed out their fault,
That a Teddy bear was suffering
And by the neck was caught.

I really did not like to see it
And little kids would be dismayed,
To see that such a cuddly toy
Was so callously displayed.

I again told them the problem
And in a shop for charity,
A bear suspended by the neck
Was not very nice to see!

Trying to use some humour
And to get right to the nub,
I told them I was chairman
Of the "Bears protection club"

The woman looked quite shaky
And could tell that I was right,
That in a shop front such as this
Should not be a grisly sight.

A manager was called to see me
From a room right out the back,
Who very soon agreed with me
That she could get the sack,
For not seeing the situation
Or the teddy bear's upset,
And very quickly released him
Saying she was in my debt!
Then starting from tomorrow
She would change the shop around,
Ensuring that all teddy bears
Would then be safe and sound.

If there's a moral to this story
It's that we must learn to care,
For each and every one of us
Starting with our teddy bear!

--ooOoo--

Splinters

Take those splinters from your posterior
You got from sitting on the fence,
As you listen and say nothing
Maybe scared you'll make no sense?
For I see you listening intently
But with no words ever said,
So if you can't venture an opinion
You may as well be dead.

Though it seems you take great care
Not to ever put yourself at odds.
So by just keeping quiet observing,
You wait to see who nods
In agreement with the others,
And not in a majority view.
Thus if you are pushed to comment
You know what to say or do.

Though some will say it's virtuous
Not to say much or express yourself,
But everyone needs at sometime
To make a statement for the health
Or progression of their brain
To keep a personality running.
But you seem to have nicely mastered
Fence sitting and clever cunning.

So take those splinters from your bum
As you come across as rather dull,
By being just a nodding puppet
Too scared to even risk a mull
Over in general conversation,
Where you may be asked to decide
If you agree or disagree,
Before you can run and hide.

--ooOoo--

A Little Loud

A while ago I wrote a poem
Which was entitled "Bar Room Star",
All about a very loud man
I'd heard in a local bar.

But recently I have met his equal
In fact he really is much worse,
With his "over the top" loud voice
That could make a vicar curse.
And I know I have said before
That I can be loud as well,
But nobody could ever equal him
With his mouth almighty hell.

Strangely he is not very big
But you wouldn't think that the case,
For the cacophony of noise he makes
Could be heard in outer space.
So no, not really very tall,
Though he has a cocky manner,
Flowing from his jaunty frame
You'd love to hit with a spanner.

Thus if a shouting contest started
I could probably hold my own,
Whist accepting I could be beaten
By blokes of twenty stone.

Though as I said he's only small
But will always be the noisy winner,
For compared to all his shouting
Anyone else is a beginner!

--ooOoo--

The "R" Word

We've all had a little falling out
Though it was quite a big deal,
When the mum used the R word
And said that the teddies weren't real!

Now I don't know how she can say that
When to me they are very alive,
Taking part in their adventures
In which they try hard and strive
To be considered as living,
And certainly they are not dead.
For being excluded from life
Is something that fills them with dread.

For Ted n Beth are very life like,
Well as much as teddy bears can.
And they don't have any presumption
Of being mistaken for man.

But the very idea they're not real
In any way, shape or form,
Makes them upset and angry
And that's what caused the storm.
As they protested and argued
That they were living and active bears.
Pointing out all their conversations
And fixing the mum with stares.

So if we are to accept they're not real
Which is extremely hard to tell,
And means that all their bear friends
Can only be toys then as well!

But I have knowledge that's certain
As any fact of life can be.
For it removes all of the doubt
When I hear them talking to me!

--ooOoo--

Booze and Two's

It is written that alcohol increases desire
But reduces performance too,
This can be proved on most weekends
When the drunkards roll into view.

Inhibitions and balance both fade
The harder they drink and revel,
With love in the air and emotions high
And skirts raised to panties level,
On young ladies mostly so serene
And always shy of the sexy scrum.
But with lots of drink inside them now
They're more than keen to flash their bum!

Blokes also will feel the effect
As more alcohol lowers their wit.
They think they're great lovers and Romeo's
But in truth most are not even fit.
Though that doesn't stop them at all
Trying to show off all their might,
With them struggling to just stand up
Let alone trying to fight!

Yes alcohol can always take it's toll
Making a fool out of me and you,
For I've never been to bed with an ugly girl
But woken up with quite a few.

--ooOoo--

Four Limericks

1

A simple young man from Kuwait
Never got to learn how to mate,
So he tried his luck
With a thirty ton truck,
And thus he sealed his fate.

2

A big fat girl named Claire
Had masses of long curly hair,
But she thought it a sin
To tuck it all in,
So now she looks like a bear.

3

A vulgar man from Dundalk
Would expose himself on his walks,
A large crow saw his tackle
And swooped with a cackle,
So now he squeaks when he talks

4

There was a frustrated young nun
Who got bored with having no fun,
So would be outrageously rude
With things that protrude,
And now has a son of a gun!

--ooOoo--

YOGA

To perform yoga is intriguing
So try it if you dare,
You sit, or lay upon a mat
And puzzle what goes where!

And when you have successfully,
Tied yourself up quite a lot,
Not moving, so it's hard to see,
If you're still alive or not?

But to help you with your yoga
And some of the pain relieve,
You lie very calm and silent,
While you still attempt to breath.

Try another skill of balance
Up on one leg, and smile,
Just practice you can do it,
But it may take quite a while!

There are though, other postures
When you just lay back and rest,
And after all the spasms,
You will like this bit the best.

Lay back and check your breathing
Going slowly in and out,
Surprisingly you feel good
And all relaxed without a doubt.

For those ancient yoga masters
Must have known just what to do,
About being calm and supple,
And living on past ninety two!

--ooOoo--

Gym Slip

Many people go to the gym
For their exercise and tone,
With some following a programme
They have worked out as their own
Best ways to keep them fit,
However much work it takes,
For the benefits are manifold
As a healthy life it makes.

But there is a little observation
That always puzzles me,
As regularly down the gym
This is what I often see,
People using the equipment
With exertion that's not slack,
But when they've finished with it
They never put it back!

Then why is this I wonder
In a place where effort rules,
Are people too bone idle
To put away their tools?
For it can't be it's too hard,
As that's the major aim,
And full activity and exercise
Are surely just the same?

So bending down to return things
Keeps floors safe and clear,
And doesn't require much effort
From fitness fans sincere.
Thus maybe as a suggestion
In their plans to keep them fit,
Should be included returning stuff
So we don't fall over it !

--ooOoo--

REFLECTION

Laurie Wilkinson

The "Walthamstow One" or The Gift?

At only fifteen years and two months
I got sent out into the world,
The very real world that is
Where "rollocking" insults are hurled.
This new place was inner London
Not where I would regularly go,
And it seemed to cause amusement
That I came from Walthamstow.

I had only just left school then
Where being older helped a lot,
But when you have to settle outside
It's a more complex plot.
For in the expanse of industry
Life can soon get very hard,
With lots to do in a decreed time
After you clock in with a card.

But I think it was the shock
Of the life to which I was strapped,
A spotty "no nothing" apprentice
Arriving naive, and all gift wrapped.
For I was youngest by a mile
Than the older and wiser males,
Who all sought to find favour
With tall stories and sordid tales.

It seemed that I was all at odds
With most of the usual view,
Though of course I didn't realise then
That most of it wasn't true.

But as a youngster you doubt yourself
Trying to mature and find your way,
So perhaps because it was easy
I was teased nearly every day.

Though I was born with a ready wit
And would answer quickly back,
Which of course did not go down well
And was told to hold my "sauce" back.
Also my natural brighter side
Was not appreciated by all there.
And especially a notable few,
But I was beginning not to care.

For as a pup grows up and gets bigger
I grew less likely to do a runner,
And till I finally got acceptance
When I landed myself a stunner,
Who I took to a work party
Held in a house nearby,
And now many of my fellow workers
Surveyed me with a green eye.

For my lady who came with me
Seemed to arouse jealousy not contrived,
And I knew that this once naive boy
Had in the grown up world arrived.

--ooOoo--

Don't Write it Off

I suppose I now have a mission
With my written thoughts in verse,
For as I scan the worldwide scene
I fear it's all getting worse.

For it seems there are wars everywhere
With the world once more on the brink.
So great leaders please take care
And give lots of time to think,
Of amazing wonders, good, and values
At new risk from conceited power.
Which can lead to mass destruction
In much less than an hour.

Of course there's been great wars before
And yet somehow we still survived.
Learning from the mushroom cloud
That insured we have now arrived,
At a state of chilling acceptance
Of just what harm man can do.
But now it seems we must again
Test out if it's all true!

So what use then is my puny verse
That on a world scale's just a jot?
But for me it's hugely important,
To give our opinions than to just not
Do anything or our make a protest,
As generations have done before.
When on monumental occasions
It did bring an end to war.

So I will scribe away my thoughts
To let my feelings be known,
As you won't succeed, if you don't try
Thus I may not stand alone!

--ooOoo--

Open Prison

Prisons don't all have bars
Like Mandela's cell so cruel.
For even with open spaces
Some confinements can still rule
The very limits of your scope
And any foray you'd like to make.
So restricted in your freedom
You feel your heart will break.

Seeing just everything you want
Or would like so much to do,
Can crack your very being
When it's all denied to you.
For if you try to journey out
Your chains won't let you go,
Yanking you back severely
With more than a physical blow.

For a soul that is so tortured
By wishes it can't enjoy,
Will be heavy, dark and rotten
From desires it can't employ.
So must look forlornly about
At scenes that appeal so much,
But remain unfulfilled and empty
From attractions it can't touch.

Thus imprisoned in a carcass
That though dead, will still breathe,
This soul will know real anguish
Caused by restraints that peeve.

--ooOoo--

Will

Well weeks will come and weeks will go
And months soon follow in life's flow.
But days we enjoy will pass by quick,
Whilst tougher times go slow.

So then we must remain steadfast
With our resolve strong and unbowed,
As all of us will have our turn
To be under a sad, tragic cloud.
For nothing in this world is given
To remain the same, or even arrive.
So grab those moments of delight
And just celebrate you're alive!

There will of course be time for sorrow
With that very time going slow,
So try to cry behind your mask
Because others may not know.

Well at least that's what I try to do
Not that I think men shouldn't cry.
But I shed my tears in private
So the world doesn't puzzle why
This chap with a constant smile
And a jokes all-day token,
May continue to laugh and grin,
When inside his heart is broken.

So back we will go to the weeks
Which pass according to our fate,
But whether going quick or slow
We should try for heaven's gate.

--ooOoo--

Just a Shadow

The visitor comes to my door
In a cloak complete with hood,
No need to ask why he's here
For that is understood.
As a shapeless face peers out
From darkness cast by shade,
So no eyes glare or gleam
To betray any offers made.

But I was quite familiar
With this figure's eerie stance,
For I had seen it many times
Though often just a glance
Of fleeting dark awareness,
And cold shivers up my spine.
Though I recognised the meaning
Of this spectre that is mine.

For in those visits to me
When no words were exchanged,
I knew temptations were offered
With safe passages arranged.
But each time I had declined
To succumb to any deal,
For my integrity and reason
My visitor knew were real.

So what you ask is the meaning
Of my visitor in sombre cloak?
And why did I deny him
The offer to remove my yoke,
Of all the burdens we carry
Which at times drive us mad?
But the answer is quite simple,
In that I chose good, not bad.

For that was the decision
My ominous caller sought,
With Siren like offers
On my very being, that he sought.
Though I am no virgin soul
Who has never made wrong calls,
But always put my hand up
If I ever broke the rules.

So no conceited hat do I wear
Or a countenance all contrite,
Just a firm unwavering belief
That I try to do what's right.

--ooOoo--

Genuine

There are two groups mostly in our lives
With people that will, and those that won't,
So the one's that won't you cope with
Unlike the "say they will" who don't.

For if someone won't do something
However much you may ask,
You know just where you stand
And must then undertake that task.
But other folks will gladly fawn
When saying "leave it all to me",
So you are left high and dry
When there are no results to see.

Now we know it's easy to talk
With little action to show,
For what they have fully promised
Is likely to be a no go.
Unlike the stiff resistive
Who just prefer to take no part,
As they have a selfish side
With no interest to even start.

So give to me a stalwart
Who will spend life trying
To succeed and really help you,
Without a thought of lying,
About what they have to do
Despite hardship and a test.
So you will have to admire them
As they always do their best.

--ooOoo--

Exposure

It takes a very brave person
To rise above the parapet alone,
And to show themselves completely
Whilst standing on their own.

Now of course they would expect
That others would support them too.
But sadly not quite the case
As some find it hard to do,
Something else for any others,
Or maybe it's indifference
That causes them to duck out
All safe behind their fence.

Of course they watch keenly
To see what happens next,
With their well rehearsed excuse
Or some other lame pretext,
That will justify themselves
From any exposure to the fray.
As they really do believe it's best
To run, and fight another day.

So what of our poor victim
Now standing open to it all?
Leading a flock who didn't follow,
And maybe smile to see him fall.
For in some cases it would suit
The cowards to say, I told you so.
We were right to keep our cover
And thus not to have a go.

Which certainly would be safer
And not take any chance to gain
Successful wins in their life,
But all their fears remain.

--ooOoo--

Begins at Home?

Bigger bugs have smaller ones
That bite them just like fleas.
And sadly now I have learnt
It's the same with charities,
Who won't embrace another
That is nothing to do with them.
Scared perhaps they'll succeed more
Which they only can condemn.

Because on asking another charity
At our local hospital setting,
If I could share with them?
But no allowance was I getting,
For a pompous do-gooder lady
Down from moral high ground stoops.
And clearly pointed out to me
They don't work with other groups!

Though she didn't seem to like it
When I replied back to her,
That it wasn't very charitable
Not to let sharing occur.
As charities should all work closely
When trying to help out all,
But still pious and opinionated
She retreated behind her wall.

Saying if other groups wanted help
They must pay like all the rest,
And I replied that's what I intend
So she wouldn't be second best,
And could actually gain from me
Whilst her charity did nowt,
But just offer my books for sale
And take their profit out!

But clearly this was unacceptable
To this blown-up, would be saint,
Who wouldn't consider others
Which as a charity, I found quaint.
So with a parting suggestion
That if all groups pulled as one,
In this unforgiving hard-nosed world
We could get more helping done.

But regretfully now I have a view
That may be hard for some to take.
But many volunteers are only doing,
Charity jobs for their own sake!

--ooOoo--

Moment in Time

The world spins on its axis
Night darkens the light of day,
Summer follows winter and spring
Our times were made that way.

Yet we go on in our existence
Even if we want to or not,
For however much we fight it
We mostly have the life we've got.
For as we continue on our road,
Days will come that bring our turn.
To have some suffering to bear,
From which we need to learn.

For as our loved ones die on us
Others will come as we see them go.
Replaced by babes newly born,
In natures continuous flow.
So enjoy what you have now
For as long as you possibly can,
Because there is no certainty
Of the time scale given to man.

Waiting for exactly the right time
To do all that you want to do,
May catch you out very badly
And be totally denied to you.
Thus best appreciate it all now
Even if the truth hurts and numbs,
For however hard to accept it
Sometimes tomorrow never comes.

--ooOoo--

Butterflies of Life

The happy butterfly is busy
Showing off its fun each day,
With many expansive shows
Of exotic scenes of play.

These conjured images of fun
Show the happy life you've got,
Being a butterfly of fun times
When in fact you're not.
For there are aches of sadness
That a loneliness compounds
Conflicting with the smiling,
As if from a wall rebounds.

For like the many comedians
Who have had a crowd in fits
Of hysterical tears and laughter,
Whilst their own life is in bits.
Struggling hard with themselves
Away from the stage and fame,
A stark inner deep reality
Illuminates their shame.

Is it like the "great Bard" said
That the lady protests too much?
With these butterflies projecting
Fun times they need to clutch
Firmly across a painted image
That smiles and doesn't cry,
Until they remove this mask
Which then shows the lie.

--ooOoo--

Pass or Fail?

Cruel echoes of a dimming past
Will hunt you down before your last
Few moments of this mortal coil,
And free you from a constant toil.

How do we receive these memories?
That seem as thick as forest trees.
Will they break our hearts in two?
Or perhaps restrain our perfect view,
That everything we did was right
Despite the haunting in the night,
And maybe make us fear our end,
The devil's angel soon may send!

Thus looking back across the years
Some of laughter and some of tears,
Will sober up any hazy thought
That in error we were never caught!
For every one of us has failed
However from this truth we sailed.

But if we didn't really seem to win
A valiant try may reduce our sin,
Perhaps absolving us from blame
If to a compromise we came,
To make an attempt to favour all
Even if causing our own downfall.

So the stepping stones of our sorrow
Will soon be healed in the morrow,
Possibly our last fading days alive
While our brain tries to contrive,
A covenant with an unerring test
That despite it all we did our best!

--ooOoo--

Pyramid

A pyramid is an ancient wonder
Of architectural progressions,
As a protective tomb for Pharaohs
When buried with their possessions,
To accompany them up to heaven
And so grace them in the after lives.
Sometimes including many slaves
Still alive, just like their wives!

Thus these ancient rulers and kings
Would have riches in a next world too,
Well that was the theory they had
But alas it was so rarely true.
For the cunning human mind
Has very few boundaries or ends,
So many of these lauded kings
Were betrayed by so-called friends.

Who ensured a secret passage or two
That would allow removal of wealth.
So after the deaths assured inside,
These valuables are taken by stealth.
Which I think gives a great example
Of man's vulnerability to sin,
And reminds us that at life's end,
We only leave with what we brought in.

So it's carbon footprints and worth,
Which will be remembered after we go.
For these can't be removed or stolen
And are left in the world to show,
Just what we did, or achieved in life
That some will just fritter away.
Like the choices and time they're given,
So they will have nothing to say.

While many folks will work tirelessly
On all of the things that they love.
Leaving behind many creations
After getting the call from above.
So can look back on a fulfilled life
Giving much to the world, and others,
Who had the joy to be with them
And embrace their life like brothers.

Thus nothing else can be taken out
Of this world, where we spend our time,
Fashioning gifts that proudly remain,
As respect and memories sublime.

--ooOoo--

Not To Reason Why

Loyal boots march where they're told
On rough terrain or forbidding ground,
For our courageous forces go
To where danger's often found.

Never to disobey or question
Any strange command given out,
No matter how they feel
Or how much that they doubt,
The wisdom of the orders
And so their best they'll try,
To perform for Queen and country
For they will just do or die.

Now these heroes all have families
Who miss them when away,
From loving parents worrying
To wives who save the day,
By keeping safe their houses
Also looking after any kids,
With school runs and homework
And preventing escaping bids.

So all of this is on the mind
Of our service personnel,
Who thinking of all those at home
Must face all kinds of hell.
From heat and dust with full kit on
To those unseen exploding mines,
Or seemingly friendly children
Who with the enemy combines.

Loyal boots march where they're told
On rough terrain or forbidding ground,
For our courageous forces go
To where danger's often found.

Now what is it we may ask
That brings so much commitment here?
With comradeship and loyalty
To those who share their beer.
But it is something more than this
Maybe not understood by me and you,
When these mixed background heroes
Decide there's a job to do!

--ooOoo--

Trying Solo

Lonely is the person
When surrounded by a crowd,
Of talking, smiling strangers
Who often laugh aloud,
At some kind of private jest
Our lonely person cannot know,
For he who goes alone
Has no shared joke to show.

So lonely is the person
Even when they're not alone,
For sometimes it is very hard
To make yourself at home.
And if in different surroundings
With another language spoken too,
However much you try to learn
It's all Greek to you.

Now lonely is the person
Sitting in a sea of sound,
And with no comprehension
No bonding can be found.
For what comes plain and simple
Each and every time we speak,
When spoken in a foreign tongue
May just as well be a squeak.

But don't be too despondent
If all washes past your ears,
For there is always a solution
So no need for your tears.
As a determined person wanting
To communicate their thought,
Can also add gesticulations
To the phrase book they have bought.

--ooOoo--

Cut Off Point

I'm having fun, and not feeling blue
But maybe due a message from you,
Though do not worry, as I surely won't.
For even if you can't, or don't
Send to me, I will not really care.
But don't be surprised if I'm not where,
You always take it that I will be
As I have many others to see.

You always wait for me to send
Another message that will end,
This communication famine time
And now my signal bell will chime.

On my new policy for the slow,
Who never reply to let me know.
If you ever got my sent email
And so don't think it's rude to fail
To acknowledge my message sent
So to end all this, I'm now hell-bent.
To eradicate the selfish few
Who won't message me anew!

Oh yes you say that your so busy
And work so hard it makes you dizzy.
But do you really think your time
Is much more important than mine?

Because if that's what you honestly think
I suggest you have a seat and think,
That just maybe you have it wrong
And you may not be healthy long,
Enough to see those later years
Ad so you'll cry indulgent tears.
Then possibly you will miss the friend
Who does no longer messages send.

So there you have it, spelt out clear
That no longer for you, will I be near,
And before you get yourself in a state
Your chance has gone, and it's too late.
Thus don't try to explain or make excuse
For you were the one like a recluse,
Who couldn't be bothered to reply,
So boogie off, I've said goodbye!

--ooOoo--

So What?

So your life is full of wonder,
And you are having so much fun,
With all the gifts bestowed on you
You surely will have won,
Every race and competition
That life can set for you.
Indeed you're a veritable paragon,
But is it all really true?

For when I hear your words
Or see what you sometimes write,
The dull ringing of cracked bells
And crowing cockerels seem to blight,
Your magnificence as an angel
Flying round mere mortals cowed,
And gathered in humbled worship
In awe as you stand proud.

So yes, we're all impressed
By the stories of your blessing,
Though the dazzle from your halo
Has us unsure, and guessing.
For "too good" normally is a warning
Not to be taken for a ride.
Though it seems you believe it all,
But maybe that's your pride.

For words said to yourself enough
Can convince your brain of them,
So you repeat them more and more
Until even your heart can't stem,
This sugary, mawkish tide
Of joy to make us jealous.
But really we aren't taken in,
By your constant need to tell us!

--ooOoo--

Effortless

The Bluebells in the woods
Proclaim the coming time of spring.
And all hopes for a bright new year
With masses of joy to bring
To your celebratory table,
Laid out for the greatest feast
Consumed by all, but especially,
Those who contribute the least.

Sawdust can clog up the works
Whilst bullshit can baffle brains.
So ensure your mind is clear
And that all the rubbish drains
From the well oiled machinery,
Running in clockwork perfection.
Thus no action or effort is required
To improve or make correction.

Bees and butterflies seem to dance
As they go about their work,
With a gusto and involvement
That many would try to shirk,
Although ensuring that for them
A lions share is obtained,
Without a hint of conscience
That in the effort they abstained.

So round and round spins the world
And fortune just a random prize,
Though often only gained by those
Who never care, or tries
To look out for any others,
Only what will effect them.
They believe that no one noticed
But watching eyes condemn.

--ooOoo--

Re Viewed

A paradox of life, and poetic licence,
With the privilege of free speech
Allows me to make all my comments,
But I must be careful not to preach
Or even drift into being pious,
Though I will always have my say.
So if you don't like my poetic views,
You can always look the other way.

For I firmly believe in expressing
My take on the world I see,
And those behaviours of people
That will amuse or enrage me.
So I observe in daily activities
All that is done or even said,
For as an expansive, prolific poet
I make sure that it is read.

At other times I really cut loose
To write what's on my mind,
About the injustice and outrages,
That in our world we find
Are often manifested by those
Sick, and psychotically converted,
To wreak horror on the innocent
After sad minds are perverted.

But mostly I love to just sit back
And silently observe what's acted out,
Daily by people of all varieties
The good, bad, thin or stout,
If involving themselves in bizarre
And strange things that they do.
So please tread soft and carefully
Or I may be writing about you.

--ooOoo--

Is it Merry Christmas?

Christmas cheer fills the world
All ready for that special day,
Got to have the greatest meal
For the best ever family day.
Smiling faces beam for the photo
All happy sat round the table.
Well mostly smiling, some just trying,
To look as happy as they're able!

For Christmas isn't all it seems
Despite your spending and the drinking,
And peace on earth, goodwill to men
Isn't really what most are thinking!

It all has to be done, put on a show
Make sure the kids presents are the best,
For when they all return to school
Their parents must pass this test.

Not much cheer in the Christmas crush
Battling each other in the shops,
To get all excesses in good time,
You must pull out all the stops.
Or be deprived of those luxuries
The adverts scream you must buy,
So your greatest day stresses soar
No matter just how hard you try.

For Christmas isn't all it seems
Despite your spending and the drinking,
And peace on earth, goodwill to men
Isn't really what most are thinking!

Greed mentality takes over dwellings
Cramming supplies up to the walls,
As if to withstand some long siege
This one day battle is made for fools
Who succumb to the media demands,
And empty their banks and cash flow.
So after the fuss and waste is done
It's not worth seeing your money go
.

But I'm no Scrooge or killjoy at all
I like a booze up too, that I must say,
Though I really can't help thinking
How nice if it was Christmas every day.
And not the seasons bloating scene
With It's pushing and shoving crowd,
Who cannot see that just being nice
All long year round is still allowed!

--ooOoo--

Ducking Stool

The Ducking Stool was a torture
From dark medieval times.
But it was also a device,
To punish those with no crimes
Other than to stand accused
By bigoted and hypocritical men,
With perverse views of law and justice,
Although it was accepted then.

For women alleged to be witches
Or men also charged with wrong,
Were ducked into water many times
Which was traumatic even if strong.
So should the victim survive this
And live somehow through the ordeal,
They were found to be guilty, and killed
Which was a cruel, unfair deal.

But no justice for the other victims
Who succumbed and were drowned.
For it had a sad and sadist irony
When innocent they were found,
By the prosecutor and court
Orchestrated by the church and rich.
Who dispensed their evil justice
For years without a hitch.

Many years on now we are civilised
Or at least that is the thought,
Though I view that with suspicion
As in traps you can be caught.

For sometimes doing the right thing
And your choice to "do or don't"
May not placate views of those,
Who damn whether you will or won't
Follow decreed lines you were told to,
As you do not believe it's right.
So that's then wrong in their eyes
And you're chastised by the might.

Of the affluent and powerful
Who obey orders like sheep, in fear
That they will always be overlooked,
Thus don't hold your opinion dear.
So just like the Ducking Stool
You may be innocent and true,
But if it offends the corrupt and liars
They seek to crush and silence you.

--ooOoo--

Life Presented in Verse

TRAGEDY

Blind Faith

Thoughts are tumbling from my head
Almost written before I've said,
What I really need to say
About our world on a given day.
With all its tragedies and war
Who knows what they're fighting for?
Just I guess, that desperate need
For more power, wealth and greed.

So little children, babes in arms
Are blown up and lose their charms,
Or any hope of normal life,
Torn away by psychotic strife,
Performed by armies of the just
Who grind opposition into dust.
Believing they have their gods will
To terrorise, maim and kill!

But this world has always seen
Acts of cruelty by the mean
And callous bullies who all say,
We must live and pray their way.
But I have hope deep in my heart
That if everyone will play a part,
We can make this a nicer place
Free of all extreme disgrace.

--ooOoo--

Accident Report

There has been an accident
At such and such a place and road.
An everyday announcement we hear
But for some the world will explode.
As spouses or family members
Or even perhaps best friends,
Could be caught up in the smash
And for some their life ends.

Thus for thousands of people each year
The accident news that was read,
Would have devastating consequences
Of serious injuries, with some dead.
Because these accidents that we hear of
Happen each and every day,
With lives changed drastically forever
Despite how hard you beg and pray.

So what causes all of these crashes
Often on roads that are mostly straight?
Well it could be drink or drugs,
Or simply someone just can't wait
Before risking a tricky manoeuvre,
Whilst some will be on their phone
But whatever is the cause
Someone could now be alone.

Of course as humans we make mistakes
In judging distances, times and speeds.
Maybe just not seeing clearly
Can be as little as it needs,
To cause life to be snuffed out
And all of us can be guilty too.
Although most won't admit to this
The facts will prove it's true.

So best to take some time out
To consider how we drive,
For with less speed and drinking
Many more people will stay alive,
Or not spend their life on crutches
Maybe with a disfigured face,
So try your best to ensure
An accident is not your disgrace.

--ooOoo--

No Milk Today

"No milk today" the bottle note said
When left for the milkman to see,
For he delivered our milk each day
Knowing what the order would be.
But sometimes if the milk built up
Or perhaps we were going away,
We had to let him know the score
With a note of no milk today.

There is though another type of milk,
That of the human loving kind.
Bestowed on others in our life
Giving strength to ties that bind
Us tight together in the world,
As we journey on our way.
Allowing giving and taking
With each other every day.

But there are days and times for me
When my understanding goes,
If contemplating liars and thieves
Along with murderers and those,
Who scar our beautiful world
With their schemes of religious greed.
Aimed at the innocents of life
Who must ensure they don't succeed.

So when these times land on me
I must indulge and apply,
The recognition and acceptance that,
My milk of kindness has run dry.
And I can't tolerate some folks
Like the moaners, frauds and crooks,
Who wish to sponge on you and me
Despite our warning looks.

So if you carry on being perverse
In what you say and believe,
With your indulgences for murder
We will make sure you leave,
The balance of our love and rights
Without a blemish from your hand.
So be prepared for foul punishment
As that's all you understand.

--ooOoo--

Come in Number Nine

Bobbing on a heaving ocean
So many miles from land,
A fragile craft of young and old
Who can't quite understand,
Why their world had imploded
Bringing death's angry flood,
To all the places that they knew
Now filled with flesh and blood.

Drifting about on an open sea
With no control it seems,
To direct this human cargo
Cast adrift to their own means.
Though this desolate water world
Is somewhat safer than their last,
With its continual rain of death
And indiscriminate metal blast.

Splashing spray now soaks the craft
Barely above the water mark,
All beneath temperamental skies
Over fear and misery stark,
With panic and a realisation stare
That a watery death and grave,
May be affected on them now
With no reward for being brave.

So why undertake a perilous cruise
Across vast waters stretching wide,
Perhaps to find wealth and fame
Or just somewhere safe to hide?
From a world changed by violent war
That no one seems to comprehend,
Even those innocent victims there
Who feared their life would end.

--ooOoo--

Hard

Life can be so desperately tough
And sometimes seems too hard,
For although trying our best to plan
We can't always choose our card.
As fortune will no doubt play a role
In deciding what's in store.
And on thinking that we've had it all
Fate will make us suffer more.

Thus as the "bard" Shakespeare said
"Worries will come not in single files,
But in battalions" all at once
Which will ensure our toughest trials.
So gird your loins, and dig in deep,
For the fight that will sorely test
You out in each and every way,
Without a break or rest!

For I once saw my stoic father broken
By the very worst of parental news,
That had fallen on me to deliver
Knowing it would cut and bruise,
These paragons of a working class
And simple values they gave to me,
That recoiled from news so severe
That it was hard for me to see.

So these tragic knocks we get at times
Can make it hard to ever recover,
And send you reeling, lost in space
As life delivers you yet another
New reversal whilst you're down,
And crushed upon your knees.
Staggering from the constant pain
That not everybody sees.

But hold on tight and steadfast
So you don't drown in your despair.
For it was never said our life was just,
And that everyone gets their share
Of the worst ever grief and woe,
Soaking you from the blackest cloud.
Yes, life can be very hard,
So stand dignified and proud.

--ooOoo--

Breached Defences

There are some kind of nightmares
That never seem to cease,
And if you cannot withstand them
You must seek for a release.
But you are bound and trapped
As the terrors raid your brain,
With horrendous visions and feelings
So you fear you'll go insane.

It's as if these invading thoughts
Know exactly where to strike,
Aware of all your hidden secrets
And those memories you dislike,
Unearthing deep regrets and guilt
You believed had gone away.
Thus now you lay still and petrified
Of what these nightmares say.

Sometimes they will fool us all
Into false beliefs and hopes.
Then crush and deny them
As your sanity hardly copes,
Whilst more dread and woe
Is visited upon your soul,
So you're transferred to certainty
Your very being is not whole.

Then these frightening nightmares
Will all your courage steal,
But more terrifying than this
Is to awake and find they're real!

--ooOoo--

Enigma

Consider all of your playing cards
And bring that cake in from the rain,
For there is always so much to do
So that you don't go insane.

If you've climbed all the mountains
But still not found your dreams,
It is looking more unlikely
That you are going where it seems
You desperately wanted to go,
And begged for in those prayers.
And this will no doubt upset you,
But no one really cares.

So walking out in the showers
And hiding from the sun,
May disguise all those tears
But not get too much done.
For Helen of Troy told lies
About something special tonight,
So the virgins trimmed their wicks
In the hope of some delight.

And as the rightful son of your father
Beware the ladies of the night parade,
Ensuring an eclipse of the sun's light
That may encompass a whole decade.
With no more sunshine ever blazing
From where it will usually shine,
Thus I worry that all the troubles
Are now going to be mine.

Yes lord I am so very thirsty,
But there's no water for you and I
That can ever quench our parched lips,
So best now that we die.

--ooOoo--

Inner Depths

I have a dark invader in me
Who tries to get into my soul,
I fight him off to keep him out
But he buries down like a mole.
So what actually is this menace?
I can't tell you as I'm not sure,
For he rarely comes to meet me
But into an abyss tries to lure.

For even the very brightest heart
Will have some darker days,
And it's at these very moments
The invader stalks and preys.
Because that is our weak link
When even fleeting doubts are cast,
As when down, problems are larger
So must be resisted until passed.

But I have an inner strength
Gained by having seen the worst
That life will throw at us,
And feeling my heart would burst.
But I now know that if I wait,
Without succumbing to the pain
Of that dour and depressive spell
My resistance I will regain.

Thus deep down inside my being
A battle is often fought,
Between my courage and dark invader
Though you may have no thought,
That all this is going on
And that I maybe losing for a while,
Because I will always look the same
And take refuge behind my smile.

--ooOoo--

Footsteps

He is a man of constant sorrow
And no pleasure can he derive,
So he really cannot care less
If he should die now, or survive.

The world he loved has broken
And shattered into many parts,
So the grief he is enduring
Would shred the stoutest hearts.

The career he loved is now over
For you have to be fully fit,
And not pain filled and crippled
Struggling to get along with it.

An unlucky placed size ten boot
On bland ground that looked fine,
Took the life he knew in seconds
With that cruel exploding mine!

It was what these heroes feared
An undiscovered explosive device,
That could rip off skin and limbs
Or cause the supreme sacrifice.
So just how do they do this job?
If wrong moves can be your end
They say you just get on and do it
With your comrades and best friend.

Now our man of constant sorrow
Begins to get on with his life,
With support of all his family
And care from a loving wife,
Who tends his hurt and fears
Like those buried deep inside.
So slowly he starts to fight back
And regain his stubborn pride.

Of course he gets help and aid
Along whatever way he goes,
From excellent support teams
That gives help to our heroes.

Thus now he has a strong lifeline
Helping his family without fuss,
So we should all help him also
Giving thanks, it's him not us!

--ooOoo--

Listen to the Flowers

There are so many people now
That won't stop to hear the flowers,
As they always rush to meetings
Or stare at a screen for hours.
Hoping to get fantastic reviews
And many more than all the rest,
Equally seeking the top ratings
Whilst yearning to be the best.

For the flowers and natures beauty
Like the birds and spreading trees,
Are still wasted on these drones
That simple things don't please.
.
As they look over their shoulders
Or battle hard to constantly reach
Peaks and heights others haven't,
As the blossoming flowers teach
Simple lessons that will arrive,
The more pressures that you stack
Upon your blind indifference,
Before you have a heart attack.

Then you can just lay back in bed
Listening to the flower's words,
To calm down and fully appreciate
All life's beauty and the birds,
Who maybe now will visit you
At your bedside window view.
For you never saw them before
And now that fact you rue.

Thus sadly your new harsh lesson
From the wonders outside your gate,
Has come to visit your suffering
So lets hope it's not too late.

--ooOoo--

Dwelling

The dwelling is totally dark
Every time that I pass by,
No lights are ever seen there
So I started to wonder why.
But the "for sale" sign gives a clue,
And has been present for a while,
For I guess there are no takers
Queuing up in waiting file.

So what I wonder is the story
Of this non-selling bungalow?
Sited in a popular area
Where properties quickly go.
But just a fleeting look outside
Doesn't fill you with desire.
And I suspect the insides too,
Won't be tempting to a buyer.

So quite likely there is a sadness
To this forlorn building here,
That has outlived its owners
Who always were sincere,
In keeping the place attractive
As once it would have been.
But no one tends it now
To keep it nice and clean.

For like all the local properties
It was kept "spick and span",
But buildings can last lifetimes
That is not a privilege for man.
So now the dark, sad bungalow
No longer has colour to spray,
Upon its gardens and contours
Since its owners passed away.

--ooOoo--

Dead

When you are dead, you're dead,
But some will die before this,
In the way they live their life
And all the things they miss
By being scared to take a chance
Or even go out on a limb.
So their chances of fulfilment
Are always pretty slim.

For death is a permanent state
That doesn't have remission,
Or any new terms of life
Even with good commission.
But we're never too sure of this
And how much of it is true,
So it's a balance for our life
With no guide of what to do.

Some are already dead inside
As they share no real emotion,
Drifting numb and bland
In a life with no commotion.
So any glow or brightness
Or a light for someone shone,
Is only a small dim beam
And very quickly gone.

But sometimes death is a failure
To express any joy or humour
With complete denial of such,
And dismissed as just a rumour.
For if sullen, sunken eyes
Lack a vibrant glint or gleam,
Then it really is impossible
To motivate a dream!

So inertia and stupefied state
Preside over lives not cherished
And even if they're attempted,
Any thoughts of life soon perished
Within this lack of activity
Or ability to share a thrill.
Thus a dire shipwrecked brain
Remains as a bitter pill.

--ooOoo--

Anaesthetise

Some times our world will break
And a splinter will cut me or you,
For however we try to deny it
The sad fact is it's true.
For however much we fight it
A pain will show up the lies,
But there is way to beat this
And that is to anaesthetise.

This though can be very tricky
As no two people are the same,
So before you seek this sanctuary
You must absolve yourself from blame,
Or any feelings of guilt
That may be piercing your shell,
As to disappear into limbo
You must choose your analgesic well.

For we will all know someone
Who has taken drugs or strong drink,
To escape their cruel world for a while
Or a break from having to think.
And perhaps see themselves differently
From the skin and suit they wear
As within this anaesthetised state
You can pretend you don't really care.

Thus nothing can touch you now
And you won't want to touch them,
Even if it's people who love you
Or perhaps those who condemn,
Your actions, words or opinion
So easy when you are still down,
But determinedly attempting to rise
And stand again without a frown.

Therefore consider those you meet
Who don't seem real as they are,
For they may be partly in hiding
So won't express themselves too far,
As that would need them to surface
From depths that protect and heal,
Giving both comfort and solace
And escape from anguish they feel.

--ooOoo--

Arrow

An arrow can be considered noble
For it is upright, straight and true,
But it also has a deadly side
With the other things that it can do.
For this slender, pointed projectile
Must be given a certain respect.
As it can be a fearsome weapon
That many do not suspect.

For fired from a bow with great power
An arrow can deliver a severe blow,
That can even pierce metal armour
And lay any poor victim low.
But more concerning than this
Is that it makes very little sound,
As it hurtles from the bow
Until hitting where it is bound.

So not only do we have a device
That can kill in a practised hand.
But often the victim won't know
Or even begin to understand
What has happened to them,
To cause such distress and pain.
Compounding all their helplessness
That they may be struck again.

But in some cases more sinister still,
The pointed barb of the end tips,
Are infected, or dipped in poison
That will spread from the place it rips.
So if the wound is not instantly fatal
Or likely to cause the victims death,
The poisoned and deadly barb
Will slowly ensure a last breath.

Now I just cannot help but consider
When mulling over these facts,
That there is a great comparison
With some people, that the arrow exacts,
In just how they will deal with others
When they decide to silently strike,
From an apparent upright, and noble look
That will conceal their spike.

So they can be quite dangerous to know
As you don't worry about turning your back.
Thinking they are benign and friendly
Until they launch their cowardly attack!

--ooOoo--

More or Less?

On occasions when I'm quiet
I peep curiously from my veil,
To survey our world starkly
And see the worried and the frail.
For time has gone by for them
With their last years running out,
So are finally forced to confront
What their life was all about.

It's so easy to be big and bold
When those years on you are few,
But life and illness take a toll
On all the things you do.
With bodies not so robust
To take the strain of days
And time spent on life's chores,
So doubts and worry plays
On those nervous thoughts,
And the changes that they fear.
Which sows more dread and woe
Until life becomes unclear.

Which leads people to a crossroad
And which path now to choose,
Between the one that says ignore
All the new things that confuse.
Or the route to try and keep up
With new technology and traits,
That get more complex daily
To leave you in dire straights.

So no great surprise that people
Get distraught in later years,
As a changing world torments them
To cry frustrated tears.

--ooOoo--

Hand of God

Scenic beauty, sweet fresh air
All you could wish for, it was all there,
For one more moment, then it was gone
When the coward set off another bomb.

Smoke and flames, cries and screams
Another end to countless dreams,
A place of wonder to melt all hearts
Was now a horror of body parts!

All be praised, his god is served
The dead just got what they deserved,
For not praying the same as those
Who blew them up and burnt their clothes.

Some strange god, that death he asks
From his army with their bloody tasks,
That spreads out terror, fear and dread
And victories measured by the dead.

Again you pray, your day is won
Religion spread by your smoking gun,
It is honour you want, your way is best,
Go tell the man with his shattered chest.

Little children, babes in arms
Now lie slaughtered with no more charms,
You say it is vengeance, we had done wrong
So we must suffer you sick death song.

It is peace you wish, and to make us sure
You continue to kill, and make more war,
Until we learn, and have passed the test
That your gentle, loving god is the best.

--ooOoo--

Lambs and Guns

I am naked except for my clothes
No match for knives, bombs and gun.
You can kill me anytime you want
For my only defence is to run.

You are fully armed to your teeth
A veritable arsenal moving on legs,
So you can slaughter and maim at will
No matter how much your victim begs,
As they relax, carefree on a beach,
At a cafe, or maybe a music hall.
Thus your foul war on the unarmed
Ensures that only the innocents fall!

Creeping, slithering, making your plans
Hiding in shadows behind a locked door.
Disgusting cowards, strapping on bombs
For your sick, ambushing war.

Thus you avoid, and wont bring to combat
Any trained and well armed man.
So you stick to putrid sewers,
And attack like only scum can.

For I am naked except for my clothes
No match against knife, bombs and gun.
You can try to kill me anytime you want,
But it's not my only defence, to run.

So stalk our free world, trying to see
Easy targets like lambs, unaware at play,
Your brainwashed mind and smoking gun
Will never earn a winners sway.

--ooOoo--

Impotent Bullies

Obscene and ungodly scum
Now copy-cats as well,
Perform their sick atrocities
That condemn them to eternal hell.

For their psychotic, twisted minds
That cannot see or understand,
Why we are free and fearless
And live in a defiant land.

So however depraved and wicked
Your cowardly acts become,
We will still revile and oppose you
And leave you looking dumb.
For nothing recently has cowed us
Or forced us to concede,
So best lose your foul ideas
Because you never will succeed.

Oh yes you've terrified people
Gang- stabbing a helpless girl,
But take a look over your shoulder
At the defiant banner we unfurl.
For you may have been scaring
Defenceless kids and unarmed folk,
But when your bomb smoke clears
You remain a sick, sad joke.

Thus employ your bully tactics
And brief moments of shed blood,
That will always curse and damn you
As a pathetic, impotent dud!

--ooOoo--

Hopeless

Heart rending scenes of anguish
Are played out around the globe,
Some may reach the media
Others we never probe,
About how dire and frightening
Are battles to stay alive.
Retreating from explosions,
Or bobbing on violent seas.
Arriving on foreign shores
Only the lucky sees.

Refugees in constant motion
Trading one horror for the next.
Old people have no comfort
With nomadic bones that vex,
Battered by cruel extremes
Of blistering sun, freezing cold.
Though mostly wet from tears,
Leaked in futile hope.
For if their plight is ever known,
None in the world will mope.

Crumbling from their traumas
With tired eyes that blankly stare
With no chance of comprehension,
Of scenes before them there,
Where a child's scream of torment
Wails futile in the winds,
That blow worse disasters near
Fuelled by man's greedy sins,
As he rages across the land,
Destroying all, gun in hand.
So suffering victims final breath
Pleads for a peaceful death.

--ooOoo--

Regrets

Bitter, dire and frustrated tears
Well up deep in saddened eyes,
As you continue to try your best
To believe in all your lies.

A shattered soul full of chagrin
Weighs heavy with your heart,
And you feel that you must mend it
But don't know where to start.

So with your whispers in the night
And dark thoughts that won't let go,
You must discover how to deal
With regrets that always show.
But first you must confront those
Easy choices when all was well.
For never giving hide or hair then,
They are now your living hell.

Such as why should you have a family
When your life was amongst stars?
As they would have constrained you,
Now that decision scars.

And with those other simple choices
Not to ruffle joyous days.
So in the dismal here and now
Bitter regret now always stays,
With realisation of head and heart
That you can never have it all,
For anytime and forever now,
And so lonely you will stall.

For you didn't want to sacrifice
Or give time and care to others.
Who now have your ideal life
When before you felt it smothers
All the things you love so much,
Or comfortable life you had.
Thus don't allow self-sorrow in,
Now your existence is so sad.

For regrets of "should have done this"
Or maybe, "I wished I'd done that".
Will haunt your lonely nights now
And make you sad and flat.

So carry on with rationalisation
But don't think that you fool me,
For regrets and misgivings now
Are in your eyes, for all to see!

--ooOoo--

Solo Flight?

We all get our individual trump
In the playing cards of life,
And that's a decision to end it all
If suffering too much strife.
Or maybe a psychotic episode
That robs our presence of mind.
Some will just want to escape justice
Leaving others with what they find.

Perhaps there is an agonising illness
That is slowly killing you.
Or depression, rejection, even failure,
And those who don't mean to,
Really complete an actual suicide
As it was just more of an act,
Of a desperation driving them,
To seek out a final pact.

So there are many different reasons
With some we never get to know,
About the life taking of people
Who determined their time to go.
So whilst maybe it's alright for them
Often there is no sign or mention,
To their family and loved ones,
About their drastic intention.

What becomes of the family then?
Bemused and bitter, left behind,
With an act that some call selfish
And at best seems to be unkind,
To loved ones picking up the mess
Of a deceased persons lifetime.
Who maybe never even noticed
Any planning for a sort of crime.

For everyone will have a view
About people deciding when to end,
Their time spent in this world
And who no longer wish to extend,
Time with spouses or family
Who won't know where to start,
To put their world back together
And mend a broken heart.

Thus some may have strong feelings
They express in a loud voice,
About their deceased loved ones
Who never got to make the choice,
Of wanting to battle on or not
And being allowed to stay.
So when families hear of suicides
It's best that they don't say,
About the internal feelings struggle
They fear might get out of hand,
For when it comes to actual suicides
They just can't understand.

--ooOoo--

Bomb

An exploding bomb's a blast of energy
Massive reaction to chemical release.
It is stunning as well as shocking
Replacing a hell on earth from peace!

An indiscrimination of violent power
A bomb spews both impact and heat,
With splintering eruption and shock
Making varied traumas hard to treat.
Shock will shatter across a body
And damage the internal organs too.
Causing cuts, infection and major burns,
Ensuring nearby survivors are very few!

Bodies ripped open by metal explosion
As projected fragments kill and maim,
Mental scars that may never heal
Should a shattered body look the same!

So we know the awesome power now
Of violence from an exploding bomb,
Made worse in confined spaces
Where living people love to throng.

Now please try hard to explain to me
The workings of an individual who,
Can callously leave such a device
Knowing the mass slaughter it will do!
--ooOoo--

Laurie Wilkinson

Appendix

Feedback on my poetry recounts that many people like to work out the meanings of my poems for themselves, and even attach their own personal experiences and thoughts. I think that is wonderful, but for other folks who like to seek my reasons and explanations for them, please review my comments below.

As I tend to write spontaneously and often on subjects that have really emoted me, I will mostly "nail my thoughts in", so most of the themes are self-explanatory. The poems listed in this appendix are the less obvious topics and thoughts, but please feel totally free to add any personalisation or meaning that they have for you individually.

Eye Line Smile:
A nice poem from my 2nd book that happened to be my first poem chosen for national publication and finals.

Volunteer:
Written on request by local Eastbourne charity organisation and read out by me to at the launch to local MP, Mayor and dignitaries.

Spark:
My description on never losing your spark for life, whatever befalls us.

The Messenger: That we should never take anyone for granted.

Faint Heart: By overcoming any faint heart you may truly find joy and delight.

Cradle to the Grave: A recognition of mothers, and included on request from my fourth book.

Fake: Be discerning of people, especially with your feelings.

Pride and Joy: Another warning not to have a faint heart in love.

Unknown Journey: Written 18 years ago but remains a favourite from my first book.

Back Pass: Always try to leave respect and love behind so that you can return without fear.

Trinket: That people are worth so much more than possessions.

Pardon: My frustration with answer-phones, especially if not saying who you've rung.

Sample:

Experiences of an essential health check that can be fraught with difficulties.

Dress Sense:

On problems of comfort and decorum.

First Sex Lessons:

Looking back at my intriguing improvisations for lack of formal sex education.

O M G!:

My thinly veiled frustrations with continued banal exclamation.

Bar Room Star:

Sentimental early favourite of mine as it was published in daily national newspaper.

Full Frontal Folly:

My sardonic take at a recent craze of people placing close up photos of themselves and expecting a fawning response.

Bear in the Window: A poem close to my heart as actually a true story, and one that people love from my very first book.

A Little Loud:

Similar to "Bar Room Star"

but notable for immense noise from a tiny person.

Booze and Two's: A firmly requested favourite from book 3 that nearly everyone agrees is amazingly true.

Yoga: Another popular poem request, especially from people who "bend" and is also on my own experiences. It was in my first book.

Gym Slip: My great amusement at "Herculean" men and women Amazons, who "work out" so hard they lack strength to return weights.

Don't Write it Off: My concerns of safety for the world with seemingly now megalomaniacs in charge of powerful nations.

Open Prison: Many people seem to me to be trapped in thought and their lives in a sort of imprisonment.

Will: This was written shortly

before publication of this book, and reflects just how quickly life can change for people, as shown by very recent events.

The Walthamstow One or The Gift?:

My painful experiences as a "spotty know nothing virgin" dunked into the cruel and cutting "real world" as a 15 year old, before gaining my strength and credibility. Amazing feedback on this poem already from people who said I had "spoken for them!" Nice!

Just a Shadow:

Like everyone else I have times of self-doubt which may come as a surprise to some people.

Genuine:

Exasperation at "all talk no do people" who often let you down.

Exposure:

Recognition that whilst some of us will give and bare all, others won't always support.

Begins at Home: Utter frustration at those "elevated" people who masquerade as charitable, but only if it suits them! They believe their charity is THE only one, and they are special so won't help others.

Moment in Time: firm favourite of mine as wonderful feedback from folks saying "so accurate and informed understanding of people struggling in life"! Humbling but proud it made national publication and finals, and is in book four.

Butterflies of Life: Falsehood and hypocrisy of people braying about their wonderful fun-filled lives, when you know that it's all untrue!

Pass or Fail?:   My second poem that made national publication and finals, and is in my third book and reflects on our lessons in life.

Pyramid: My recognition that who we are and what we do in life will be the only "possessions" left behind in life.

Not To Reason Why: Recognising our wonderful armed forces and their families.

Trying Solo: On despairing loneliness when amongst crowds and people.

Cut Off Point: About so called friends who only bother to communicate when they need something. Ring any bells?

So What?: Another look at people who brag "too much" about their wonderful lives, seemingly unaware of everyone else's contempt and disbelief.

Effortless: Possibly my modern take on "The 3 Little Pigs" with people happy to be passengers of life and contribute nothing.

Re Viewed: In life today we are often "on camera", so now perhaps another proclamation that I, and others are watching too.

IS It Merry Christmas?:
My caustic and sardonic view of what Christmas is like for many. I must have made my point as also published nationally and in their finals.

Ducking Stool:
Another observation that in life you can't always win and maybe "damned if you do, and damned if you don't".

Accident Report:
A look behind the bland statement we mostly hear every day on traffic news, "there has been an accident"...

Blind Faith:
A light of hope in face of now almost regular bad news.

No Milk Today:
That sometimes it is very hard to understand or forgive.

Come in Number Nine:
Thoughts of why people risk great dangers at sea.

Hard:
Life can be very hard at times, but we must try to deal with it.

<u>Breached Defences:</u> That we all have demons that we must meet head on.

<u>Enigma:</u> I had twice tried to write an abstract poem but they both turned into quite profound poems. This is for everyone to make fit for them.

<u>Inner Depths:</u> Everybody has their vulnerable "down times" in lesser or larger ways, as I do too. This poem explains my resistance.

<u>Bomb:</u> Poem from my 3rd book that has taken on more meaning in recent events, and describes the awful effects of a bomb in confined spaces. Has just been published nationally and also in their finals.

<u>Footsteps:</u> Much requested and again from book 3 this poem is a tribute to our courageous armed forces and their sacrifices. Also about the people who look after them.

Listen to the Flowers: For people maybe too wrapped up in their ambitious striving, that they don't fully appreciate the world.

Dwelling: A simple, but I think quite profound poem, on my seeing a bungalow near me going into decline and failing to sell. I wonder about the people who used to live in it.

Dead: We all die become dead, but some seem almost dead when alive.

Anaesthetise: My view that when sad or hard times hit us, we must find a way to get through, or "anaesthetise" ourselves for protection.

Arrow: A suggestion that all people who look harmlessly genuine, aren't.

More or Less?: That you must attempt to keep up with a complex and changing world as you get older, or else you may become more cut off.

Hand of God:

One of the first poems I wrote over 3 years ago when I became a more prolific poet. Often requested for its simple but powerful message about not using religion as a vehicle for terror.

Lambs and Guns:

Another of my poems published and in finals nationally. I wrote it after the November 2015 Paris terror atrocity.

Impotent Bullies:

Written in anger following two terror attacks in Manchester and then London.

Hopeless:

On the increasing number of refugees having to desperately flee their homes in panic and fear, after they had become war zones.

Regrets:

A bit of a double slant on people who have deep regrets in older life, but try hard to cover them up, but fool nobody.

Solo flight: Maybe an apt poem to end the main text of this book. Having worked closely with desperate, depressed and suicidal people, it is my review of how and why people consider and complete suicide.

More?

I hope that you enjoyed this book
For I tried to pack lots in,
With various themes in sections
So you can choose where to begin,
And take yourself on journeys
Or if you wished to, just remain.
For I have other books out now,
Thus you can have it all again.

With poems to make you romantic
And some verses if you feel deep.
Others will make you look back on life,
Even smile when you go to sleep.

Of course Ted and Beth will feature
I can hardly leave them out.
As surely they'll have new adventures,
Well of this I have no doubt!
And I will have new observations
I glean from scanning life's tree.
Take care then you are not included
When I write down what I see.

So please look at my other books
And support "Help for Heroes" too,
For all my sales donate to them
From my poems I write for you.

You can get books from my website online
And to message me direct will be fine.
With every contact listed below
Including all that you need to know,
To search for me on the Amazon club
Or just come and find me down the pub!

My books are Poetic Views of Life
MORE Poetic Views of Life,
Reviews of Life in Verse
And Life Scene in Verse.
So all of these books are mine,
But are now growing all the time!

My contacts:-
Email = lw1800@hotmail.co.uk
Amazon authors page = Laurie Wilkinson
Facebook page = The Psychy Poet Laurie
Wilkinson Website = www.psychy.com

Laurie Wilkinson

Lightning Source UK Ltd.
Milton Keynes UK
UKOW04f1059130817

307196UK00001B/42/P